FORGIVENESS

*Overcome the Past to
Be Christlike in the Present*

ROY DANIEL

CONJURSKE PUBLICATIONS

*Rhinelander, WI
2016*

©2016 Conjurske Publications

All rights reserved. Published 2016.

ISBN-13: 978-1-935923-03-9

Conjurske Publications

3215 County Rd G

Rhinelander, WI 54501

www.conjurskepublications.com

Printed in the United States of America.

TO EZRA BRAINARD,

a very good friend.

Contents

Foreword . . . . *vii*

Preface . . . . *ix*

WHY WE FORGIVE 11
God's Expectations for Christians

WHAT WE FORGIVE 19
The Causes of Bitterness

CONSEQUENCES OF BITTERNESS 29
The Outflow of Unforgiveness

HOW TO FORGIVE 43
Biblical Freedom from a Bitter Heart

LIVING LIKE JESUS 67
The Outflow of Forgiveness

THE NEXT STEP 81
Horizontal and Vertical Relationships

FOREWORD

To forgive is difficult. Our hearts may whisper, "To forgive is impossible!" Peter in despair asked, "How many times shall I forgive my brother?" His words reflect our thoughts on so many occasions. Forgiveness is a decision of the mind to forget, to wipe out, and to not hold a grudge against another. Forgiveness is the tool that enables you to show love to the person who faces you as an enemy. Forgiveness is not placing yourself in danger: at all times, we must be "wise as serpents and harmless as doves." Forgiveness starts in our heart and then reaches out to other people's hearts. Roy Daniel tackles a hidden cause of failure in the home, church, and workplace. He focuses on the need to forgive and places in our hands the practical, Biblical methods to implement it.

You will not be able to put the book down. At the end, your cry will change to "Lord, I forgive!"

Jannie le Roux

(Grandfather of Roy M. Daniel)

PREFACE

In my travels around the world, I have heard various sermons and read many books and articles on forgiveness. I have seen bitterness destroy families and churches alike. By God's grace alone, I have also been able to introduce many people to powerful Biblical principles that can set them free from the chains of resentment. This book uses real-life illustrations and provides practical, applicable, and Biblical principles to guide the Christian toward forgivenes. By God's grace, it bursts open God's truths in a heart-warming way. Whether you struggle with bitterness, desire to help someone else, or know someone bitter towards you, it will make you laugh at yourself and cry before God. This book is not about the author, but about the will and means of the Lamb that was slain: Jesus Christ.

Roy Daniel

Why We Forgive

GOD'S EXPECTATIONS FOR CHRISTIANS

Thousands of symbolic white crosses cover a monumental hill in Ysterberg, South Africa, placed there in memory of murdered farmers. Farm attacks are common in this country, often leading to rape and murder. One Sunday, a car stopped outside the house of a farmer I knew while he was leaving for church, and a few people got out and told him to remain quiet. He replied that he had no time for nonsense and was late for church. As the farmer walked back into the house, they shouted "Stop!" He spotted a gun in the car window and shouted to his wife to lock herself in her room. An instant later, a shot rang out. As the farmer collapsed, he managed to reach for his pepper spray and use it to send the shooter away howling. My bleeding friend called a neighbor and told him about the assault. Surrounding farmers rushed to the area, caught the attackers, and took them to jail.

While in the hospital, the injured farmer struggled with

the question, "Why did they do this?" Even as a Christian, he felt angry and bitter. Just before falling into a semi-coma, he made the amazing choice to forgive. As he told me later, at that moment God felt so near, and his heart was free in the knowledge he had utterly forgiven his attackers. The men ended up in jail unable to hurt more people. The farmer they shot was not an enemy, and he had no desire in his heart for revenge. The doctors said the internal damage was so bad, he should not have survived. However, after an extended hospital stay, he was released to go home.

We live in a real world with real problems. Churches and families split, young people are molested, family members die, people are betrayed, promises are broken, money is scarce, health is lost, and Satan rubs it all in.

What should our heart's attitude be when we have been wronged?

Mark 11:26: *But if ye do not forgive, neither will your Father which is in heaven forgive your trespasses.* (King James Version)

JOSEPH'S BROTHERS

All around the world, I have frequently heard messages on forgiveness that reference Genesis 30–50, the amazing story of Joseph's forgiveness toward his brothers. God told Joseph in dreams that his family would one day bow down to him. When Joseph told his brothers of these dreams, they became jealous and cruel toward him. His brothers threw him into a pit to die, then changed their minds and sold him to passing Egyptian slave traders. In Egypt, the traders sold him to a rich merchant called Potiphar. Joseph experienced success for a while, until Potiphar's wife dragged his name through the mud by falsely accusing him of raping her. Potiphar had him thrown into prison. Through all this, God's word was trying him, and he did not become bitter.

Psalm 105:17–19: *He sent a man before them, even Joseph, who was sold for a servant: Whose feet they hurt with fetters: he was laid in iron: Until the time that his word came: the word of the LORD tried him.*

God had given Joseph a promise. But for years, he lived through what seemed to be the opposite of that promise. Joseph could either accuse God as a liar, or he could continue to trust God in spite of his circumstances. Throughout this period of trial, he chose to believe in God. Eventually, the fulfillment of God's word came, and Joseph became second-in-command of Egypt. During this time, there was a great drought and Joseph's brothers came to Egypt looking for food. They stood before the man they had greatly harmed without recognizing him, due to his clothing and his use of an interpreter. Joseph held the power to punish them severely, yet as he observed the change in their attitudes, he chose instead to forgive them and treat them well. He told them later, "But as for you, ye thought evil against me; but God meant it unto good, to bring to pass, as it is this day, to save much people alive." (Genesis 50:20)

Joseph forgave much, recognizing that God was in control even when others had done him wrong. But because Joseph only expressed his forgiveness outwardly after his brothers had shown their remorse, some interpret this to mean they need only forgive people who are already sorry themselves. They may say, "God only expects me to forgive those who ask me for forgiveness." Or, "God only forgives repentant people, so why should I forgive someone who does not see his wrong nor is willing to change?" But this reasoning is flawed; I knew a missionary who would only forgive those who requested it. A friend of mine went to visit him after he retired. He came back broken-hearted, saying "All I see in his eyes is bitterness."

> *Joseph forgave much, recognizing that God was in control.*

JESUS CHRIST ON CALVARY

Jesus Christ—God manifest in the flesh—made the decision to forgive His unrepentant murderers while dying as the substitute for our sins. With a crown of thorns on His head and blood dripping from his hands and feet, He cried "Forgive them, for they know not what they do."

Luke 23:34: *Then said Jesus, Father, forgive them; for they know not what they do. And they parted his raiment, and cast lots.*

One day, Jesus will sit as Judge over the world. But two thousand years ago, He walked on earth as our example of how we as humans should live toward God and others.

Romans 12:19-20: *Dearly beloved, avenge not yourselves, but rather give place unto wrath: for it is written, Vengeance is mine; I will repay, saith the Lord. Therefore if thine enemy hunger, feed him; if he thirst, give him drink: for in so doing thou shalt heap coals of fire on his head.*

While we can tell people their sins are evil, we cannot personally hold those sins against them. We can stand up for God, but we must not hold personal grudges against others. Jesus was our example on the cross:

> *A thorn crown on His head,*
> *A sinner by each side*
> *Our Saviour cried, "Forgive!"*
> *Just before He died.*

Some people may say, "That was Jesus. I am just a human, and God does not expect the rest of humanity to forgive unrepentant people." But let us look at a man in the New Testament who was stoned to death for preaching truth.

STEPHEN'S DEATH

Acts 7:59–60: *And they stoned Stephen, calling upon God, and saying, Lord Jesus, receive my spirit. And he kneeled down, and cried with a loud voice, Lord; lay not this sin to their charge. And when he had said this, he fell asleep.*

Amazingly, here was a mere man whose death mirrored Christ's in two ways. Firstly, he asked God to receive his spirit, just as Jesus did.

Luke 23:46: *And when Jesus had cried with a loud voice, he said, Father, into thy hands I commend my spirit: and having said thus, he gave up the ghost.*

Secondly, Stephen asked God to forgive the unrepentant men who were stoning him to death. He is a clear example of a man choosing to follow Christ and forgive in a way that the world will not.

> *The wind and the seas obey Him. Do we?*

Mark 11:26: *But if ye do not forgive, neither will your Father which is in heaven forgive your trespasses.*

The wind and the seas obey Him. Do we?

Bitterness in any degree always results in spiritual harm. While saved and unsaved people alike can become bitter, a Christian will experience serious problems in his relationship with God when he allows bitterness into his life. As you progress through this book, you will learn how to forgive based on the finished work of Christ. I will explain the "what, when, why, and how" of forgiveness from a God-centered, Biblical perspective. Furthermore, I will explore the damage of bitterness, the freedom of forgiveness, and the resulting journey toward Christlikeness.

What We Forgive

THE CAUSES OF BITTERNESS

What makes us bitter? We are going to look at a few illustrations of what causes grudges in a person's life. While bitterness is often associated with horrendous crimes such as murder, the fact is people can be bitter about anything—Jonah was even bitter about a plant.

Jonah 4:9: *And God said to Jonah, Doest thou well to be angry for the gourd? And he said, I do well to be angry, even unto death.*

TRIVIALITIES

In Natal, South Africa, a dentist told us about a Zulu person who had come to him with a toothache and asked for the tooth to be pulled. Because he had built up bitterness against the painful tooth and wanted revenge, he took the extracted tooth home and smashed it with a stone.

FAMILY

As a teenager, I was sometimes tempted to hold resentment against my dear father over the most trivial issues. One day, for example, he asked me to make my bed even though I was already intending to do so. Another time, he requested I wear a suit to a school event. When I arrived, I was the only one wearing a suit. Despite the fact my father was amazing and understanding in every way, my sinful nature desired to become bitter over the smallest offenses. I have met many other young people who have told me in tears that they cannot forgive their parents for requiring them to perform such basic duties as bathing or cleaning their bedroom.

But on the more serious side, other youth are bitter because their parents fail to keep their promises or spend time with them. I met a girl at a camp in South Africa who blamed herself for her parents' fighting. Her bitterness led her into completely rebellious living that eventually devastated her life.

SELF

People often struggle to forgive themselves. Years ago, Stafford Finnimore was the chaplain of Durban Central Prison. By God's grace, he brought many prisoners to a saving knowledge of Jesus Christ. One day, two prisoners sat before him, and one seemed to break through to God while the other struggled in darkness.

Finnimore asked the second man, "Do you believe God can forgive you?"

"Yes!" the man replied.

"Can you forgive yourself?"

"No."

"There is your problem!" Finnimore explained.

When we don't forgive ourselves for past failures, it is as bad as when we don't forgive others. Some blame themselves for their parents' divorce. The fact is, you may or may not have been part of the problem, but bitterness against yourself does not answer the problem. It only adds to your sin.

Many people are bitter against their bodies because they think they are ugly. They cannot forgive the mirror for what they see. One pretty girl told me that half her face was ugly. "Which half?" I asked, as both halves looked fine to me. She didn't have a reply for that. When someone tells me they are ugly, I tell them to get a new mirror: essentially, a different attitude. Since beauty is in the eye of the beholder, everyone has some form of beauty. Some have bodies that have been damaged through accidents or ravaged by bad health, but in the end it is the beauty of the heart that counts. Absalom impressed men with his attractiveness, but to heaven he was odious. In contrast, Isaiah 53 states that there is no outer beauty in Christ that we should desire Him; beauty radiates from inside His being. One day when we see Jesus, we will receive perfect, new bodies. Right now, God expects Christlikeness of us, which includes contentment with ourselves and our appearance.

Hebrews 13:5: *Let your conversation be without covetousness; and be content with such things as ye have: for he hath said, I will never leave thee, nor forsake thee.*

Bitterness against ourselves is actually bitterness against God. He is the one who made us what we are and places us in the circumstances with which we are discontent. You may think it is acceptable to be bitter at yourself, but it is actually both selfish and prideful. Contentment does not mean neglecting yourself by not combing your hair, brushing your teeth, or taking your medication. You can maintain and improve your body out of self-respect without being discontent about what you cannot change.

BROKEN PROMISES

Often people become bitter when others let them down. Once while on the mission field, I needed money to complete a project. I had been promised the money by someone before the project was finished, so in anticipation of that I had spent months on this particular undertaking. Unfortunately, by the time the money was needed, the donator had changed his mind. It was tempting not only to feel disappointment but also to disobey God and become bitter.

> *Bitterness against ourselves is actually bitterness against God.*

Once, a wealthy man got excited about a message I preached and invited me to preach in his town, promising to arrange wonderful meetings. Two evangelist friends and I spent hours preparing, but when we arrived, nothing had been arranged. Money was scarce, and we had to hitch a ride with a local missionary because we ran out of petrol. My friends were assigned to Christian homes that did not offer them food, while I stayed with the man who had invited us. He made me spend ten hours working outside, painting a wall while my feet bled from walking on embedded glass. It was a struggle to not become bitter; one of my coworkers in particular was quite angry with him. We needed grace to make the decision to show love anyway. In the end, God worked in his heart and he provided us with money, petrol, and food.

HISTORICAL INJUSTICE

Hundreds of years ago in medieval society, daily life often involved feuds. For example, someone would steal another knight's shoes. The knight would retaliate by burning that person's crop or stealing his daughter. Each knight would teach his children bitterness by retelling the story of the other man's wrong. Seven generations later, the great-great-great-great-grandchildren would still be told the story. If someone had just stopped retelling the story, the feud would have ended.

Managing the memories and information from the past can be a risky process. In South Africa, the government, schools, and media remind people of past injustices. They say, "Remember what the colonialists did to the Africans." Interestingly, the general consensus is that children born after colonial oppression had ended are, on average, angrier than those who actually experienced it. Learning about the past can be more detrimental than the past itself. Other African countries with similar oppressive histories often do not share the same level of bitterness, because the government chooses to live in the present rather than the past.

FINANCIAL PROBLEMS AND HEALTH

Financial loss, health problems, and death are frequent causes of bitterness. Even those who follow Christ wholeheartedly will find it hard to resist bitterness when someone they love suffers or dies. But consider examples of those who have faced such challenges and overcome the temptation towards bitterness. Elisabeth Elliot's husband, Jim Elliot, was killed by people he tried to reach for Christ. She did not become bitter but went back to preach the love of Christ to the same murderers.

My grandfather, a farmer, often experienced financial difficulties. Once he came close to ruin by spraying every other tree with insecticide, causing 35,000 of his citrus trees to die. During financial stress like this, his electricity and telephone lines would get cut off because of unpaid bills. During one such crisis, when it was touch-and-go as to whether he would lose everything, a stranger came to visit. Without mentioning his own troubles, my grandfather told the man of salvation through Jesus Christ.

Jesus Himself, while dying on the cross, took time to lead the man next to Him to salvation. Even under those terrible circumstances, Jesus showed selflessness. But bitterness will lead to selfishness, preventing Christlikeness in such moments.

MISUNDERSTANDINGS

People can become bitter over things that never happened, such as misperceptions about the motive behind another person's actions. Others can make a mountain out of a molehill, or hold a grudge because they mistake the facts. When I was in Bible college, I was convinced through a number of circumstances that my tuition money had been stolen. As it turned out, I was completely misinformed, the evidence vaporized, and I learned that the money had reached the proper person after all.

The next illustration is the cherry on the cake, showing how we can allow bitterness over the smallest trivialities. In South Africa, the older generation of Afrikaners believe that younger people should be the first to greet elders. This practice is good and respectful, but not Biblical law. Once while at a Christian camp, I absent-mindedly walked past an older, well-known preacher without greeting him. As an English South African, I did not always remember this Afrikaner practice. After walking by, I heard a harsh shout behind me.

"Why did you not shake my hand, young man?"

Startled, I asked, "Didn't I?" and moved on without giving it much thought.

Two years later, I was asked to be the main speaker at a

conference this preacher was attending. I had heard he had been used of God through his preaching. When I saw him at the conference, I thought, "I want to learn from that man." He told me later that after seeing me, his thought had been, "What a proud brat!"

God worked among the people as I preached that evening; with tears in their eyes they sought to repent of sin and make right with Him. When the workers came together for prayer the next morning, this preacher sat and cried.

"For the past two years," he confessed, "I have been bitter because Roy did not greet me at a camp we both attended. God has broken my heart, and I do not want to stand in the way of His work." I sat there amazed; all this time, he was the only one that had been affected by his bitterness.

> *Unforgiveness can be compared to drinking the cup of poison that you have prepared for another.*

At that point, another worker spoke up. "Sir," he said, pointing at the older preacher, "While we are on this topic, I want to confess my own bitterness towards you over the past several years."

"All these bitter people," I thought. "Yet in this case, I was not affected."

Unforgiveness can be compared to drinking the cup of poison that you have prepared for another. Later on, we will examine the Biblical harm that is inflicted when we refuse to forgive.

DISCONTENTMENT TOWARD GOD

Regardless of the cause of bitterness, it is always ultimately directed at God who provided our looks or allowed our circumstances. Discontentment about the circumstances in which God has placed you is actually bitterness against Him who set you there. Satan sowed discontentment in Adam and Eve's lives even while they lived in paradise, telling Eve that God was withholding fruit from them. They rebelled against God, and the earth was cursed for their sin. If Satan is clever enough to convince people in paradise to be discontent, how much more ammunition does he have in today's cursed world to sow discontentment and bitterness towards God!

Consequences of Bitterness

THE OUTFLOW OF UNFORGIVENESS

The first consequence of unforgiveness, apart from losing close fellowship with God, is the surrender of ground to Satan.

Ephesians 4:26–27: *Be ye angry, and sin not: let not the sun go down upon your wrath: Neither give place to the devil.*

Anger is a natural impulse that we have to deal with if we are to become Christlike. However, it is interesting that God does not utterly condemn us for every time we feel disappointed, irritated, or angry. God tells us to not let the sun go down on our wrath, and then He says:

Ephesians 4:31: *Let all bitterness, and wrath, and anger, and clamour, and evil speaking, be put away from you, with all malice:*

If we are commanded to lay aside anger, why does verse 26 seem to condone it? God knows that in the path to Christlikeness, we will fail at times and become irritated or angry.

Even when we may think we are justified, we must keep these feelings contained. Anger should not be allowed to gain control of our emotions. We should deal with anger by yielding our rights, resting in Christ's finished work, walking in faith, and allowing time for growth. It is very important to realize that becoming angry at yourself for prior failures is not the answer, but only adds to the problem. Keep in mind that sometimes, these failures are simply the result of lacking sleep or exercise. Taking care of ourselves on a physical level should not be forgotten while maintaining spiritual health.

> *A key indicator between anger and bitterness is time.*

When we do become angry, we should not sin further by allowing it to settle into bitterness, because failure leads to more failure. I remember getting irritated with a friend quite a few times, but we always forgave one another and were best pals again. It was wrong, but it did not become deeply-rooted bitterness. Over time as we grew in Christ, we had fewer and fewer heated debates, choosing instead to obey Christ's command to lay aside anger. If you choose not to forgive, then you have become bitter. A key indicator between anger and bitterness is time; if you wake up in the morning still angry about yesterday's conflict, you are allowing a grudge to take root.

FORGIVENESS

Satan is able to gain place in your life when you become bitter. The Greek definition for *place* in Ephesians 4:27 means *jurisdiction*—which is an area of your soul in which Satan can work and harm you spiritually. Satan's jurisdiction over a person varies in its level of severity. In Africa, we have people who are demon-possessed, while others simply have epileptic attacks which can be mistaken for demonic possession. However, there is a third group of people who are so given over to bitterness that they can appear possessed. The devil has much ground to work on, which leads to demonic oppression. You can continue to cast the demons out, but it will not lead to lasting freedom. The bitterness just allows them the right to come back again and again.

During a men's prayer meeting, several elders were struggling to help one man who was suffering from demonic oppression. "Get off of my back," he would yell as they urged him to 'pray through'. This continued for hours with no success, until a visiting preacher asked for permission to briefly talk to the man. In desperation, they assented.

"Is there anyone you would refuse to recognize if you saw them coming down the street?" the preacher asked.

"No—except the man I have a lawsuit against."

Those praying around him reacted in shock. "Unless you

are willing to deal with your bitterness," they told him, "you will never be free."

THE TORMENT OF UNFORGIVENESS

2 Corinthians 10:4–5: *(For the weapons of our warfare are not carnal, but mighty through God to the pulling down of strong holds;) Casting down imaginations, and every high thing that exalteth itself against the knowledge of God, and bringing into captivity every thought to the obedience of Christ;*

Some very godly people like to take the verses in Ephesians 4:26 and link them to 2 Corinthians 10:4–5. They then make a doctrine stating that lies leading to disobedience against God always appear on ground that has been given over to Satan through bitterness. However, taking two unrelated verses and linking them in this way to form a separate doctrine is a practice that cults do freely. When a group does this, they create a fixed and specific meaning that may not be related to the main point of either passage. In much the same way, Christians sometimes use these two verses together to teach that a person who has given ground over to Satan will of necessity believe his lies. But while bitterness can at times cloud a Christian's judgment and lead to discernment issues, this is a principle rather than a Biblical rule. Others dealing with bitterness may never experience this problem. But what we do clearly know from Scripture is that a bitter person will eventually suffer under God's tormentors.

Matthew 18:34: *And his lord was wroth, and delivered him to the tormentors, till he should pay all that was due unto him.*

To understand this verse we have to look at the context. In Matthew 18:21–35, Peter asked Jesus how many times a man should forgive a brother. Peter thought himself generous to mention the number seven. Jesus stunned him by answering "seventy times seven". Using a parable, He went on to explain why Christians should freely forgive others.

Jesus told of a king who had a servant that owed him ten thousand talents—a fortune. The king called the servant and ordered him to pay, but unfortunately, the servant could not. So the king commanded that he be sold as punishment, along with his wife, his children, and all that he had. The man fell down and worshipped him, begging for more time.

Born as descendants of Adam, this is a picture of every human being. We have a debt we cannot possibly pay. We have not only been born with a sinful nature that desires to live without the only true God, but we have also broken God's holy law. If it was a man's law that said, "Thou shalt not lie," breaking it would not be so bad. Every man has lied at some time, and therefore no one can judge others harshly without judging themselves. God, however, is perfect, and He can judge in a way that man views as harsh without condemning Himself. By telling a lie, we have not sinned against man, but against a holy God. The punishment is in accordance with who He is. Who we are and what we have done is eternally evil in God's eyes. No number of good works will provide compensation to appease God's wrath over our sin. It does not matter if we have broken one law or all the laws; we owe a debt so great we could never pay it. All we can do is fall down, acknowledge Him as God, and beg for mercy. Mercy by definition is something we do not deserve, and this is exactly what God grants us.

Proverbs 20:28: *Mercy and truth preserve the king: and his throne is upholden by mercy.*

The parable goes on and tells how the king, a picture of God, proved himself worthy of the title by showing mercy. He freely forgave the man for what he could not pay if he tried, setting him free from his awful debt.

That is what God does when we come to Him, humbled enough to surrender, asking Him in faith for mercy. At that moment of repentance, God forgives us freely. He can do this righteously, because Jesus died in our place for our sins and then rose again on the third day. The problem is that some people forget what they deserve. They carry on as if they are a perfect example of God, never needing mercy.

In the parable, we see this servant had a fellow servant that owed him very little, only 100 pence. Instead of forgiving the man who also asked for mercy, he threw him into prison.

A friend of mine in South Africa owed about $200 to another Christian. Instead of holding this against him, his friend chose to release him from the debt. The parallel created in both these stories compares the concept of debt to that of forgiveness. Just as a creditor can write off a debt, so forgiveness is a choice to release others from the debt of sin we feel they owe us.

We have to realize that under the law, we deserve hell. Every sinful action performed against us is a sinner hurting someone who has sinned. This is nothing compared to what we deserve in hell for the smallest sin against God. In the eyes of society, sin is only evil to the degree the person sinned against is good. For example, to kill Hitler would be considered heroic, but to kill Mother Theresa would be abominable.

This principle can be applied to sin against God, who is the embodiment of perfect good. Anything done against God Himself is far worse than the greatest sin committed against a fellow man. But for grace, even the worst any man can do against you is just a small part of what you deserve. To take God's place by holding judgment against another is self-idolatry, for at that point we are setting ourselves over God. When you are bitter, you are forgetting God's holiness and the greatness of His own forgiveness towards us.

Continuing the parable, the lord heard of his cruelty and lack of forgiveness:

Matthew 18:32–35: *Then his lord, after that he had called him, said unto him, O thou wicked servant, I forgave thee all that debt, because thou desiredst me: Shouldest not thou also have had compassion on thy fellowservant, even as I had pity on thee? And his lord was wroth, and delivered him to the tormentors, till he should pay all that was due unto him. So likewise shall my heavenly Father do also unto you, if ye from your hearts forgive not every one his brother their trespasses.*

Regardless of what you believe these tormentors to be, they are a very serious matter. Even if they do not keep you from the gates of heaven, they will certainly torment you throughout life. We have the power in Christ to escape those tormentors and obtain the peace of God ruling in our hearts. However, bitterness robs us of the joy and peace we could have in believing.

Ephesians 4:31: *Let all bitterness, and wrath, and anger, and clamour, and evil speaking, be put away from you, with all malice:*

If you allow the sun to go down on your wrath, you could be tormented by depression, envy, and more. God allows the ground given over to Satan to be used as punishment for your wrong attitude, and you will be tormented. Many Christians live in varying degrees of torment, depending on the depth and time length of their bitterness. Now, some people may have physical problems that cause depression, and forgiving may not remove their need for medication. Nonetheless, they must still forgive anyone against whom they hold bitterness.

Like children, we may need discipline to help motivate us. But we should not be like a child who stops being rude simply to escape spankings, while believing in his heart that his rudeness is not wrong. We should not forgive only to escape tormentors, but also because bitterness is sin against the God we love.

> *To take God's place by holding judgment against another is self-idolatry*

EFFECTS OF BITTERNESS ON OURSELVES

I knew a blind South African preacher who quoted Scripture contextually in a wonderful way. He once told the story of someone who held bitterness against him for a long time. Eventually, the man forgave him and came to tell him so. The blind man laughed and replied, "You don't have to apologize to me. You have not affected me by being bitter for the last few years; I could not even see that you were cross with me. The only person you have been hurting is yourself."

Bitterness is sin against the God we love.

You can read about many "spite houses" on the internet, which are built solely to provoke neighbors. A famous example of this is the Richardson Spite House, built in 1882 in New York City. Joseph Richardson owned a narrow strip of land which was comparatively useless for development. When the owner of the adjacent plot, Hyman Sarner, offered to add it to his own plot for $1000, Richardson refused such a low price and set out to prove that the land could be used for construction. He built a narrow house on the property, measuring four stories tall, but only five feet wide. The sad thing is that this house was so narrow and impractical, all it really did was spite Sarner by blocking his view. Richardson and others like him actually live in the prison of their own spite, still believing they have "won". Spiritually, when we are revengeful toward others, we are often just imprisoning ourselves.

EFFECTS OF BITTERNESS ON OTHERS

Although many times the only person you hurt is yourself, in other cases bitterness will also affect others. Cain, the first baby, grew up and murdered his brother. Because God accepted the sacrifice of Abel his brother and rejected his own sacrifice, Cain became bitter and jealous, which led to his brother's death. Clearly, Cain's bitterness had fatal consequences in another person's life.

Many Christians have been used of God for years as missionaries and preachers, but later in life they become bitter and hurt others. Either by direct attack or whispered backstabbing, they try to destroy other Christians' names and often succeed. Truly, bitterness can impact those around us.

Hebrews 12:15: *Looking diligently lest any man fail of the grace of God; lest any root of bitterness springing up trouble you, and thereby many be defiled;*

God warns that bitterness can spread to others. I remember one Bible college student who expressed his bitterness by much complaining, infecting many students with his attitude. Others, however, displayed a powerful testimony by resisting his influence and keeping their eyes on Jesus, causing others to become positive as well. Either your bitterness or your positive attitude can affect your church, work place, and family.

40

It is natural to react without love toward those who show none. Even more so, it is possible to become very bitter against such people. This bitterness can affect others, including your children. I have visited the homes of many preachers and missionaries, and have seen how people tried to destroy them from within their own church fellowship, denomination, or mission group. Most will find these situations difficult and experience normal struggles. Unfortunately, some will allow the struggle to deepen into bitterness which they display in front of their children by their conversation and actions. Others sought God for grace to speak with love about those that did them wrong. Remarkably, a higher percentage of children raised in such cases later became missionaries themselves. In the first instance, however, many children desire to have nothing to do with their parents' organization because they had been taught to live with bitterness.

I have often witnessed two people go through the same fire in life. One person becomes hard and bitter, while the other becomes soft and more like Christ. You play a part in the way you develop.

Once while traveling to a zoo with my wife and sister-in-law, my GPS led me through terrible traffic in the middle of the Pretoria City District. Crowded streets can be dangerous in such areas, so I told them to shut their windows while leaving mine open. A poor man came by and patted my chest, asking for money. I told him to get his hand out, but he ignored me and I became angry. He then saw my cell phone and snatched it. I grabbed his arm and we struggled, but he got away. I was angry and flustered, so it took a minute to jam open the car door. Once I got out, I looked around and saw someone running who slowed down to a normal walk. I left the ladies alone—stupid, angry me—and ran after the man. I tackled him to the ground, but he insisted he was the wrong man. He said he knew the thief and would go get my cell phone for me, but of course, he never returned.

It is amazing how your feelings on the surface can tell you everything is fine when there is actually a spiritual problem in your heart. The fun things in life may feel good while you experience them. As I looked at the monkeys and elephants that day, I felt happy. I did not realize that a hook of bitterness had pierced my heart; I had to find that out later.

> *I was not overcoming the past to be Christlike in the present*

During the next few weeks, every time I saw a beggar, especially at traffic lights, I would not only close the car window but also wave my arm and loudly snarl, "Get away!" One day, I saw such a beggar walking toward my car. I hissed and waved my arms, but then his eyes broke my heart. They held no anger, just dead hopelessness. It was as if he was thinking, "You are just another man who does not love me." As I drove on, I cried. I realized I was not overcoming the past to be Christlike in the present. God gave His Son to die for His enemies, yet I would not love my fellow man because of a stolen cell phone.

Next, we examine the answer to bitterness—and it is sweet!

How We Forgive

BIBLICAL FREEDOM FROM A BITTER HEART

Forgiveness begins when we ask God to forgive our own bitterness. This step is necessary but not sufficient; we must also trust Him for the grace to choose forgiveness. Choosing to forgive can be hard, but it is made possible based on God's work at Calvary. We can and must choose to release the people we are bitter against from the debt we think they owe us. The strength to do this comes from God and His finished work, and we can trust Him to complete the process of emotional healing that follows the act of forgiveness.

REDEMPTION

When we allow ourselves to linger in anger, jealousy, or hurt through bitterness, we become ensnared by it. We do not have the power in ourselves to overcome it. What can we do? The answer is based on the principle of redemption.

Fanny Crosby, who went blind six weeks after birth, never

remembered having sight. However, instead of becoming bitter, she only wished to have been *born* blind so that the first person she saw would have been Jesus. She died on February 12, 1915 after she had written over 8000 hymns that touched the hearts of millions. The secret to her victory was based on her understanding of the Biblical principle of redemption.

The first stanza of her hymn "Redeemed" reads:

Redeemed, how I love to proclaim it!
Redeemed by the blood of the Lamb;
Redeemed through His infinite mercy,
His child and forever I am.

She also wrote "I Shall Know Him":

When my lifework is ended, and I cross the swelling tide,
When the bright and glorious morning I shall see;
I shall know my Redeemer when I reach the other side,
And His smile will be the first to welcome me.

Chorus:

I shall know Him, I shall know Him,
And redeemed by His side I shall stand,
I shall know Him, I shall know Him
By the print of the nails in His hand.

Redemption means we are purchased out of slavery, but what does that involve on a practical level? Sinners are enslaved to sin and its consequences. God paid the price to set us free. In doing this, He bought us out of slavery and redeemed us. While some live as if this means we are bought by God to be our own master, this is not the case.

In the Old Testament, the Passover is a picture of Christ's redemptive work. When the Israelites were slaves in Egypt, Pharaoh refused God's command to let them go, so God sent ten plagues. For the last plague, God declared that all the firstborns in Egypt who did not put the blood of a lamb on their door posts would die. When God's judgment came that night, it only passed over those firstborns protected by the blood. Interestingly, God did not consider these saved firstborns as set free from slavery so that they could do their own thing, but instead considered them His sons:

Exodus 13:2: *Sanctify unto me all the firstborn, whatsoever openeth the womb among the children of Israel, both of man and of beast: it is mine.*

Numbers 3:13: *Because all the firstborn are mine; for on the day that I smote all the firstborn in the land of Egypt I hallowed unto me all the firstborn in Israel, both man and beast: mine shall they be: I am the LORD.*

This applied not only to the firstborns that survived the plague, but to all firstborns from that point on. The firstborn of cattle had to be sacrificed as a gift to God, and every firstborn of man had to be acknowledged by a payment to God. God said He would swap His property, the firstborn, for the entire Levitical tribe. They would then serve Him utterly and devotedly as His property.

Numbers 3:41: *And thou shalt take the Levites for me (I am the LORD) instead of all the firstborn among the children of Israel; and the cattle of the Levites instead of all the firstlings among the cattle of the children of Israel.*

GRACE FROM REDEMPTION

Everything is God's property through creation, and for that reason we should honor Him. However, we cannot because our human hearts are owned and enslaved by sin. Jesus came as our Passover Lamb and redeemed us by His sacrifice, thereby providing the opportunity of freedom from the bondage of sin to be His property. We are His property: not only because He created us, but also because He has purchased us with His own blood. And in the same way that He expected the Levites to serve Him because they were His, He also expects us to serve Him because we are not our own.

> *Grace is not a license to sin but freedom from a life of sin*

Some say this principle only applies to the Old Testament. After the cross, they claim, we can do what we want with ourselves because Jesus died to set us free. We can do our own thing and be our own master. They call this freedom in Christ; "being under grace". But this sort of grace is a disgrace.

Titus 2:11–13: *For the grace of God that bringeth salvation hath appeared to all men, Teaching us that, denying ungodliness and worldly lusts, we should live soberly, righteously, and godly, in this present world; Looking for that blessed hope, and the glorious appearing of the great God and our Saviour Jesus Christ;*

God's grace teaches us to live godly and deny worldly lusts, not to do our own thing under an umbrella of false grace. Grace is freely available in Christ and sets us free from the power of sin—something the law cannot do. However, it is not a license to sin but freedom *from* a life of sin, changing us from corrupt to Christlike. This transformation begins at salvation and continues through our Christian life. When He returns, we shall be like Him and shall see Him as He is.

All of this is based on redemption: God's purchase of us as His property through Jesus' finished work on the cross. Ponder for a while the following verses:

1 Corinthians 5:7b: ... *For even Christ our passover is sacrificed for us:*

1 Corinthians 6:19–20: *What? know ye not that your body is the temple of the Holy Ghost which is in you, which ye have of God, and ye are not your own? For ye are bought with* *a price: therefore glorify God in your body, and in your spirit, which are God's.*

Your body and your spirit are the property of God. This is just like the redemption concept in the Old Testament, but with deeper spiritual implications. Bitterness is firstly a sin against God, and it is also a snare you cannot set yourself free from. Only God can restore you based on the finished work of Calvary where He bought and redeemed you.

As God's property, we must consider both the aspect of our responsibility and the reality of His power.

PERSONAL RESPONSIBILITY

We cannot do what we want with our body and heart under an umbrella of grace. God is holy, and we should attempt to walk holy through grace. God lives in us, calling our body His temple, and therefore we should keep ourselves clean. We cannot abuse grace by using it as a license to sin—whether in the material we read and watch, the things we listen to, the places we visit, or the activities we do. A desire to misuse God's grace in this way is a sign that we have either backslidden or are not saved. We cannot claim to follow Jesus while living in iniquity, for iniquity means to live without God and pursue our own ways.

Concerning the Judgment Day, Jesus says:

Matthew 7:21–23: *Not every one that saith unto me, Lord, Lord, shall enter into the kingdom of heaven; but he that doeth the will of my Father which is in heaven. Many will say to me in that day, Lord, Lord, have we not prophesied in thy name? and in thy name have cast out devils? and in thy name done many wonderful works? And then will I profess unto them, I never knew you: depart from me, ye that work iniquity.*

People who believe they have freedom to sin under false grace will never enter Heaven. Now, it is possible for a Christian to sin, since salvation does not produce perfection. We will not be perfect until we reach Heaven and receive our new bodies. God's grace in our hearts teaches us not to sin, drawing us toward Christlikeness and away from looseness. Jesus is near to help us up when we sin—if we are humbled by it, for *"God resisteth the proud, and giveth grace to the humble."* (1 Pet. 5:5) We should not wake up each morning thinking, "I can enjoy sin today because of grace." This demonstrates that we neither know nor love God.

Romans 6:13–14: *Neither yield ye your members as instruments of unrighteousness unto sin: but yield yourselves unto God, as those that are alive from the dead, and your members as instruments of righteousness unto God. For sin shall not have* *dominion over you: for ye are not under the law, but under grace.*

God wants us to yield the members of our body—eyes, ears, hands, and feet—to do right. The law cannot overcome the power of sin in our lives, but grace can. Keeping the law on the outside cannot overcome the spiritual problems on the inside, but Jesus can by His grace.

> *Christianity is a religion of the heart—not consisting of a creed, but of life found in the person of Christ.*

Christianity is a religion of the heart—not consisting of a creed, but of life found in the person of Christ.

Galatians 6:14: *But God forbid that I should glory, save in the cross of our Lord Jesus Christ, by whom the world is crucified unto me, and I unto the world.*

Paul recognized that keeping the law outwardly would not give him the inner power to live a holy life. Not only the forgiveness of sins, but also the power to be Christlike is based on God's finished work at Calvary. He realized it was only in and through Christ that he could be crucified to the world. Although the body must be kept under subjection because its natural desires can clash with God's word, he did not chastise it as sinful. Rather, Paul acknowledged that his strength was based in Christ and His finished redemptive work.

GOD'S POWER

As God's property, we have more than a personal responsibility: we also possess the privilege of Christ's power working through us. For example, allowing the sun to go down on our wrath gives Satan the jurisdiction to play on God's property. But because of Christ's finished work on Calvary, God as Owner has the authority to tell Satan to leave—and he must go. You can struggle to make him leave yourself, but just as we were not saved by works, we cannot use works to attain spiritual victory either. You need Jesus to cleanse you and kick Satan off. Thus with excitement I bring your attention to the following verse:

Mark 11:25: *And when ye stand praying, forgive, if ye have ought against any: that your Father also which is in heaven may forgive you your trespasses.*

I have often wondered about this verse. Why does God tell us, while *standing* and praying, to forgive? God does not honor a specific position, as the Bible speaks of many prayers answered that were spoken from all kinds of stances. Perhaps this is because we tend to sit, kneel, or walk for long prayers, but for quick prayers we may just stand still for a minute. Essentially, God is saying that forgiveness is not an emotional work, for we have been bought at Calvary. We don't have to cry for hours, working up feelings until we have impressed God with our penitence. This would be like climbing a mountain to add to the work of the cross. Because of His finished work, God can cleanse us and take back lost spiritual ground in a moment. Long prayers or fancy words are not required; we can choose to forgive in simplicity and ask God to cleanse us and take back the lost ground. Our faith is not in words or works, but in the person of Jesus Christ. When we have a problem and come to God for the answer, He can powerfully undo in a moment what Satan has gradually destroyed.

Now, the process of emotional healing takes time; it is not necessarily an amazing sensation of immediate forgiveness. Emotions can take time to catch up with God's work, but they will do so as we trust and God heals. It is important to note that God does this work Himself, through the Lord Jesus Christ. God knows your struggles and is willing to be the loving, practical answer to your needs.

DEALING WITH MEMORIES

I picked up a conservative Christian magazine once and read an article on forgiveness. It stated that if you have not utterly forgotten, you have not forgiven. The author based this on the fact that when God forgives, He removes your sin as far as the east is from the west. The article quoted these verses:

Hebrews 8:12: *For I will be merciful to their unrighteousness, and their sins and their iniquities will I remember no more.*

Hebrews 10:17: *And their sins and iniquities will I remember no more.*

Many expect us to be like God and forget those who have wronged us. But Paul was able to list the actions, places, and people involved for any time that he had been tortured or his authority rejected. For example:

2 Corinthians 11:24–28: *Of the Jews five times received I forty stripes save one. Thrice was I beaten with rods, once was I stoned, thrice I suffered shipwreck, a night and a day I have been in the deep; In journeyings often, in perils of waters, in perils of robbers, in perils by mine own countrymen, in perils by the heathen, in perils in the city, in perils in the wilderness, in perils in the sea, in perils among false brethren; In weariness and painfulness, in watchings often, in hunger and thirst, in fastings often, in cold and nakedness. Beside those things that are without, that which cometh upon me daily, the care of all the churches.*

> *Our faith is not in words or works, but in the person of Jesus Christ.*

Paul was right with God, yet he still remembered these circumstances without holding a grudge against anyone. With all respect, forgiveness is not Alzheimer's. It is not what you remember, but how you remember. I remember someone smacking me in the face years ago; yet I have a free heart towards him and have enjoyed his company since. This can make people feel they can never forgive, because they happen to have a brain with basic memory functions. While it is not good to focus on past negatives, it is going beyond God's word to have to not only forgive but also forget the memory.

In a way, even God remembers sin: God knows every verse in the Bible, signifying that He "remembers" the recorded sins of saints who were later forgiven. For example, God forgave Peter after he denied Him three times, yet the deed is still recorded.

God does not remind us of the past to condemn us. If you are in Christ, He has completely removed your sins. He knows they happened, but they have been erased from His judgment list. When God forgives someone, He accepts him as washed in Christ's blood and justified as though he had never sinned. In Christ, he is a guiltless child of God with a new heart. Hallelujah!

SATAN'S USE OF MEMORY

Our ability to remember does bring up a problem. Satan is aware of past hurts, and he knows what to target to bring those emotions back. Sometimes after praying to forgive, we immediately experience an emotional freedom that lasts forever. But in other cases, we are only free for a while before the hurtful memories and emotions return. We are then tempted to become bitter again or think the cross is not enough.

> *Forgiveness is not what you remember, but how you remember.*

Let me note one thing. Some people can easily get huge victories over major offenses, yet struggle to forgive small things. Perhaps this is because small annoyances build up numerically, or it may depend on how much they either love or hate the one who hurt them. Possibly it is simply from letting the guard down when faced with smaller, "less important" issues. If we choose beforehand to make forgiveness a habit, these situations can be handled more easily. An "attitude of forgiveness" has helped many people. Nonetheless, even when this attitude is present, situations occur where emotions are provoked, and the temptation toward bitterness increases.

How do we Biblically handle the lingering emotions resulting from these conflicts? Firstly, recognize that feelings may take time to catch up with the decision to forgive. Sadness is not necessarily bitterness; you can weep over your child's death without becoming bitter. But remember that many times, both elements are present. God sets us free from bitterness immediately, but will take longer to complete the emotional healing of our heart.

Secondly, we should obey God's word. Forgiveness is not the chief end in itself; inner victory can be attained by making the deliberate choice of obedience. But after we make this choice, we must go still further. It is not enough to simply forgive; we must choose to show love by blessing our enemies. By going this "extra mile" of obedience, we can ultimately find healing even when emotional victory does not come immediately.

THE STRUGGLE OF FORGIVENESS

Years ago, a godly man who commanded great influence and respect across South Africa decided I was terrible and should leave the mission field. He phoned influential people to tell them this, and since he was so godly and respected, what he said carried much weight. He tried to destroy my name, possibly believing that he was doing the right thing. Now, I am not a brilliant preacher. But since God in His mercy saved me, I live to tell others of what Christ can do for them.

This man had enough power to destroy my ministry for a lifetime. I sat on my bed and shivered in fear, unable to understand. I prayed and asked God to take back the ground Satan had captured in my heart. I felt alright for a few seconds, but then the anger and confusion would return as I thought of what was happening. Suddenly, I had a simple thought. How can I love an enemy if I never had one? I realized that some verses in the Bible can only be obeyed when God allows things to go wrong.

Matthew 5:44-45: *But I say unto you, Love your enemies, bless them that curse you, do good to them that hate you, and pray for them which despitefully use you, and persecute you; That ye may be the children of your Father which is in heaven: for he maketh his sun to rise on the evil and on the good, and sendeth rain on the just and on the unjust.*

Luke 6:27-28: *But I say unto you which hear, Love your enemies, do good to them which hate you, Bless them that curse you, and pray for them which despitefully use you.*

Once we obey the Scriptures' command to love our enemies, God often provides emotional victory. Sitting there on the bed, I decided to look to God for grace. I knelt down and asked God to bless his family, wife, children, and work—and I meant it. It was then that the peace and emotional freedom came. Every time I feel tempted to be bitter, I try to remember to pray for my enemy's good, and victory comes. God does not command anything for which He will not also provide grace. I later became good friends with the preacher who tried to destroy me. This will not happen every time; how they treat you after you have forgiven them is their own responsibility before God. Nonetheless, you must forgive.

> *God does not command anything for which He will not also provide grace.*

Job went through many terrible circumstances in which he lost his family, possessions, and health. His friends told him such things could only happen because he was a sinner. Job could have been tempted to be bitter against them because they attacked his integrity. But instead, he chose to obey God and pray for his friends' good. Once he did, God removed his inflictions and blessed Job with far more than before.

Job 42:10: *And the LORD turned the captivity of Job, when he prayed for his friends: also the LORD gave Job twice as much as he had before.*

While visiting a godly older lady, I picked up her notebook and read an old saying. "All Heaven stands still when someone prays for his enemy's good." Does Heaven ever stand still for your prayers?

Sometimes, I remind myself how little people have done against me compared to what man did against Christ on the tree. It was not the nails that put Him there, but my sin and your sin. Although He had all the power of heaven at His command, He allowed Himself to die for man's salvation.

The struggle to forgive isn't always a one-time thing. Many people live with a difficult spouse or work in an environment filled with anger and mistreatment. Life is not easy, but God expects us to have a daily attitude of forgiveness. We may fail at times, but we must get up and face the right direction. We should take the opportunities to forgive that God gives us, using them to become a powerful testimony for His name.

It is not wrong for a person to remove themselves from a difficult situation when possible. This is not necessarily an option for a spouse, though of course one must use common sense and seek help in situations

> "All Heaven stands still when someone prays for his enemy's good."

HOW TO FORGIVE

involving abuse or other extreme circumstances. But when the difficulty is in the workplace, it is not wrong for a person to change employment when possible. This change, however, must never be an alternative to forgiveness. Jesus said:

Matthew 10:23: *But when they persecute you in this city, flee ye into another: for verily I say unto you, Ye shall not have gone over the cities of Israel, till the Son of man be come.*

DECEPTIVE DESTROYERS

Some destroyers appear friendly and sow discord among the brethren with a smile. If a perceptive Christian tries to gently warn an undiscerning bystander without describing the destroyer's sin, the bystander may retaliate by questioning his intentions and labelling him as bitter. Eventually, the bystander falls into the trap of bitterness himself—first against the Christian who warned him, and then against the destroyer once he realizes his true intentions.

We must be careful believing what people say about others. We also need to beware of men like Absalom who win people's trust with their smiles and seemingly positive attitudes. Sometimes people believe the Absaloms and distrust the Jeremiahs who warn against evil. Using discernment can help protect us against the temptation to bitterness that is sure to follow if Absalom deceives us. Nonetheless, even when we suspect that a man may not be sincere in his kindness toward us, we can still be good to him. To be good to someone when you don't know their true attitude towards you is blindness, but to be good to someone when you know they despise you is kindness.

PRACTICAL FORGIVENESS

Some people are impractical when it comes to forgiveness. In the Bible, God not only talks of faith but also of wisdom. We should use our common sense so far as it does not cross Scripture. People who do not check their car's oil, believing God will take care of it, will find that their car fails. One lady I know, who spent approximately fifty years as a missionary, was known for great devotion but little common sense. One time, early on in her missionary career, she remarked to a coworker that she did not need to use a torch since the Lord was her light. While walking across a field at night, she fell into a hole. Her coworker asked her, "Where is your light now?"

Practical Christianity indicates we do not necessarily have to trust everyone we forgive. We must show love to all, but we should only trust those who are worthy of trust. If someone has murdered one child, though we must forgive him, we should not offer him a room alone with another child. Leaving $200 in a room with someone who has just stolen money would be tempting that person in the name of forgiveness, and that is wrong.

Matthew 10:16: *Behold, I send you forth as sheep in the midst of wolves: be ye therefore wise as serpents, and harmless as doves.*

When we come to God humbled over our sins, a wonderful thing happens. He forgives us, changes our heart, and trusts us with a renewed oneness with God. We should keep our hearts for God, as His trust in us is a huge privilege and responsibility. But God's trust in a humbled, forgiven sinner whose heart has changed is not the same as our trust in an unrepentant murderer. We need not trust wicked people, but rather love and forgive them much as Stephen loved and forgave his murderers.

A SENSE OF HUMOR

A lady I knew who daily endured stress and mistreatment once remarked, "The only way I survived without bitterness was through God and a sense of humor." God created us with a need for humor. Some monkeys that I have seen in Africa are so fearfully and funnily made, their main purpose must have been to make us chuckle. When I look at the mirror in the morning, I could feel irritated about my appearance, but it is better to laugh.

God is not a joke—He sends people to hell. My point is not to justify ministers who are clowns rather than servants of God, flippantly joking about holy things. But pure humor is not wrong. Spurgeon said, "I sometimes tickle my oyster until he opens his shell, and then I slip the knife in."[1] In the Bible, such men of God as Elijah used sarcasm towards the prophets of Baal. Paul did the same.

A soft answer turns away wrath, and some men are able to do the same with a good dose of humor. Even a child can choose to laugh instead of becoming bitter. A young man that I knew could make his mother laugh when she got angry. Once, she was very upset with him and his sister, and she yelled "that's enough!" over and over until the poor little girl was ready to cry. Her brother started to laugh, causing his mother to laugh too and realize how wrong she had been to yell instead of disciplining with a controlled spirit. Of course this will not work in every situation; some parents may interpret laughter as mocking, and other times it wouldn't be

---

1   Charles Spurgeon, *The Soul Winner* (New York; Chicago: Fleming H. Revell, 1895).

appropriate. Nonetheless, humor could work to alleviate the temptation towards bitterness.

FORGIVENESS AND REPROOF

What if my child is rude to his mother and tells me I cannot discipline him because I preach forgiveness? I would tell him to bend over, and I would give him something to forgive me for. I would not smack him out of revenge or hatred, but give him what he needs to correct him in love. Parents who scream at their children in bitter anger while disciplining them are wrong. Nonetheless, parents who discipline their children in love are Biblically correct.

Proverbs 23:14: *Thou shalt beat him with the rod, and shalt deliver his soul from hell.*

Of course, the purpose of discipline is to assist children in doing right, not to beat them until they are blue and bleeding. In God's eyes and in the eyes of most societies, this type of treatment is wrong. But sadly, some people throw away basic discipline because of the actions of minority extremists.

At an appropriate time, we should explain to a homosexual or a thief why we disapprove of their sin. But we should always speak the truth in love. Some people enjoy reproving people out of spite rather than grace. We must avoid this unloving attitude and forgive personal grievances without overlooking sin against God. But speaking the truth in love is impossible if we harbor bitterness.

> *The absence of bitterness does not equal the presence of true salvation.*

Ephesians 4:15: *But speaking the truth in love, may grow up into him in all things, which is the head, even Christ:*

Some who do not know Christ still appear to have forgiven a great deal. Political prisoners and others who suffered at the hands of cruel men have used will power to endure intense suffering without extreme bitterness. But the absence of bitterness does not equal the presence of true salvation. Neither is it necessarily the same as the heart-felt forgiveness God enables Christians to display. If a man seems to forgive but continues in a life of sin—whether as a religious hypocrite or a supporter of abortion, homosexuality, and other wickedness—he is no friend of God. If you have never truly met with God, then forgiveness will ultimately count for nothing on Judgment Day.[2]

---

[2] Visit www.uwitness.net/scc for an excellent message on how to know you are a Christian forgiven by God. "Salvation Crystal Clear" by Jerry Mawhorr.

Living Like Jesus

THE OUTFLOW OF FORGIVENESS

"To Be like Jesus" is an old, famous hymn that describes what the Christian's supreme desire should be. When God saves us, He does not just give us a ticket to Heaven, but also a new heart that loves Him. Religious Pharisees did not have a new heart that desired to be like the Biblical Jesus. While they possessed an outer shell of works, their inner nature had not been renewed. It is natural for unsaved people to love those that love them. God, however, expects and empowers Christians to love their enemies. Doing good to those we love is easy; it is far harder to extend kindness without ulterior motives to those who have wronged us.

LIVING WITHOUT REVENGE

Years ago, I failed as a missionary and shouted angrily at my superior. He responded in Christlikeness by reprimanding me, then went to our mission counsel and told them, "I have never met someone as submissive as Roy." He ignored my one big failure and focused on the months I had been mostly submissive. I was amazed when I heard this. If Christ and His servants are so patient with me, how much more should I also love and forgive those who wrong me?

Matthew 18:21–22: *Then came Peter to him, and said, Lord, how oft shall my brother sin against me, and I forgive him? till seven times? Jesus saith unto him, I say not unto thee, Until seven times: but, Until seventy times seven.*

Seven is the number symbolizing perfection, so Peter essentially asked, "Do you expect us to forgive perfectly?" Christ responds by asking Christians to go seventy times beyond the number that man calls the symbol of perfect forgiveness. This does not mean we are to forgive only 490 times, and then we can be bitter and vengeful to people who hurt us. Jesus taught that we are to truly forgive people from the heart, giving up any desire for revenge.

KINDNESS TO ALL

I have learned that I must be kind to people who smile to my face but lie behind my back and do much harm—not just once, but again and again. I seek God for grace to do this as each opportunity arises. Each new lie will hurt, but God grants fresh grace each time this happens until responding with kindness becomes a joy. At times, God will allow trouble so He can reverse the situation for His glory. We will not always see that glory until we reach Heaven—but the wait is still worth it. However, taking our eyes off Jesus will cause us to miss all of this.

Occasionally we will need to correct wrong information. But we must not rely on people believing the facts, for our source of life is Christ. Although difficult, we should remind ourselves of this important concept when we feel depressed. If lies were to spread, I am not afraid of informing certain people about the correct information. But it must be done in love for the purpose of protecting ministry, not to retaliate against the person who lied. Paul did not attack those who attacked him, but he did correct false information when necessary (Acts 24:21).

In some cases, defending ourselves with the truth can do harm to many others. At such times, it can be better to "live down" the lies told against us. A faithful Christian life will confuse those who have believed the falsehoods. They will walk away shaking their heads, wondering how someone so "evil" can possess such peace and joy. Perhaps they will even discern the truth about the situation, but even if they do not,

LIVING LIKE JESUS

we can bear it if our eyes are truly on Jesus. God knows the whole situation, accepts us despite our mistakes, and will set everything right on the Day of Judgment. Faith in this truth will give Christians the strength to smile at those who have reviled them.

Matthew 5:11-12: *Blessed are ye, when men shall revile you, and persecute you, and shall say all manner of evil against you falsely, for my sake. Rejoice, and be exceeding glad: for great is your reward in heaven: for so persecuted they the prophets which were before you.*

According to Andrew Murray, "A believer may pass through much affliction, and yet secure but little blessing from it all. Abiding in Christ is the secret of securing all that the Father meant the chastisement to bring us."[1]

When I fail in this regard, Satan is there urging me to give up. In contrast, Jesus stands near saying, "Get up and follow me." Despite our failures we can get up and forgive, looking to Christ to love through us by abiding in Him and His finished work.

---

1 Andrew Murray, *Abide in Christ: Thoughts on the Blessed Life of Fellowship with the Son of God* (Chicago; London: Fleming H. Revell, 1895).

PRACTICAL LOVE

Some people have so many enemies that it is impractical to do good to all of them. I know people who wronged me years ago, but I am too busy with evangelism, Christian websites, books, and mission work to find them again and show them grace. God will sometimes take people out of our lives, or we simply move away from the people who have hurt us. If someone hurts your family, you should forgive them on a spiritual level. But for the sake of your family, you should also cut ties with them in love.

But in other cases, God allows a person to remain prominent in your everyday life—perhaps a fellow missionary, family member, or coworker. You should show tangible love toward them again and again. The selfish heart does not want to do this, but it is possible through Christ. God dealt not only with the guilt of sin, but also with the power of self through Christ's death. If we know Jesus, we don't need a new experience to be victorious; we simply rest in the person of Jesus Christ. In Him, we can experience what He did for us at Calvary. We will make mistakes, but we can't say we don't have the power we need. When I fail, it

> *When I fail, it is my own fault; when I am victorious, it is Jesus.*

is my own fault; when I am victorious, it is Jesus.

Some believe God is wrong to expect us to love our enemies. They say there are many good things in the Bible, but God should have skipped that impractical command. But I thank God that command is in the Bible. If He did not love His own enemies, He would have never sent His Son to die for us and we would end our lives in hell. God loves His enemies, and He expects us to do the same.

God is not only good to Christians, but also shows love to the unsaved. For example:

- He sent His Son to die for His enemies while they did not love Him.

    Romans 5:7–8: *For scarcely for a righteous man will one die: yet peradventure for a good man some would even dare to die. But God commendeth his love toward us, in that, while we were yet sinners, Christ died for us.*

- God allows sinners to live when all they deserve is hell. It is only by His love that sinners are alive and have the chance to hear truth each day.

    2 Peter 3:9: *The Lord is not slack concerning his promise, as some men count slackness; but is longsuffering to us-ward, not willing that any should perish, but that all should come to repentance.*

- God sends blessings such as sunshine and rain to all people, both friend and enemy alike.

    Matthew 5:44–45: *But I say unto you, Love your enemies, bless them that curse you, do good to them that hate you, and pray for them which despitefully use you, and persecute you; That ye may be the children of your Father which is in heaven: for he maketh his sun to rise on the evil and on the good, and sendeth rain on the just and on the unjust.*

    Just as God sends rain to those who hate Him, so we should also love our enemies. God is the Judge of all men, and will preside over the whole earth on Judgment Day. Nonetheless, God is love and shows His enemies goodness in many ways they don't deserve. Since we are not God, vengeance is not our property. We must tell the truth about sin while showing only love towards the sinner. But neither are we to stand in the way of government and justice; we must always exercise practical common sense. Just as many of God's enemies despise His goodness toward them, so they will also despise us.

    Romans 2:4: *Or despisest thou the riches of his goodness and forbearance and longsuffering; not knowing that the goodness of God leadeth thee to repentance?*

    While a man lives, God's heart desires that he will repent of his sinfulness and place his faith in Him.

2 Peter 3:9: *The Lord is not slack concerning his promise, as some men count slackness; but is longsuffering to us-ward, not willing that any should perish, but that all should come to repentance.*

A gift is anything we have which we don't deserve. We deserve only hell, thus all good we possess is a gift from God for which we ought to be grateful. We never have any right to be bitter against Him, for our abilities to see, breathe, walk, and listen are gifts. That is why God expects those who do not have as much as others to be thankful and content. Our circumstances should not be compared to what other men have, but rather to what we deserve. Improving our circumstances is fine if we are content with the rate at which God blesses our efforts.

> *We must tell the truth about sin while showing only love towards the sinner.*

A PECULIAR PEOPLE

The world is accustomed to benevolence toward charities and kindness toward friends. What would it take to *really* have a testimony for Christ?

Titus 2:14: *Who gave himself for us, that he might redeem us from all iniquity, and purify unto himself a peculiar people, zealous of good works.*

FORGIVENESS

A famous Christian in China was accused of stealing money by people he secretly supported financially. What would you do in this situation? While most would stop their support, he continued to anonymously assist them. Only after his death did they discover who had been helping them.

Most people will immediately stop supporting a missionary who has gossiped about them. This is human nature, but not God's peculiar love. A close friend of mine continues to give anonymously, even when missionaries gossip about him. Sometimes he will share the truth with them if it is of practical help, but regardless of their response, he goes on giving. Amen!

ERIC LIDDELL

Eric Liddell is famous for his refusal to run in an Olympics race scheduled on a Sunday, out of respect for the Lord's Day. What fewer people realize is that he did not love the spotlight. At the height of his fame he went to China as a missionary, leaving the limelight for God's light. He met his wife Florence soon afterwards, and together they had two girls. As a result of World War II, conditions in North China became quite dangerous for foreigners. Eric sent his pregnant wife and children back to her family in Canada, expecting to follow them within a year. Unfortunately, after Japan's attack on Pearl Harbor, the Japanese occupying North China began treating all foreigners as enemies. Eric, along with hundreds of other children and adults, was sent into a concentration camp with very little food or basic necessities. Many died, including children and those who were weak or ill.

Eric believed that in whatever situation God places a person, one must live without resentment in content surrender to His will. Many people can change their circumstances from job to job or town to town, but Eric could not. Often God chooses to hold us where we are, even for a short time, in the expectation that we will live in this surrender. Of course we shouldn't be afraid to improve our situation if we are able, but never at the cost of disobeying His word—and never out of bitterness. If we do not surrender, we become bitter and cannot obey His word. Active surrender is leaving the results in His hands and accepting His specific decision. God wants us to rest in the fact that He is in control.

Eric surrendered daily, seeking God for grace to love the Japanese while making himself a blessing in the concentration camp. He actively made himself useful, teaching school and playing games with the children. When he met a boy without shoes, Eric gave the boy his own.

A few Christians in the camp began meeting for Bible study. During one of these meetings, they discussed the Biblical principle of loving our enemies—specifically, the Japanese. Did God actually expect the Christians to *love* them? One man said the goal itself was unachievable; they could only strive towards it. Eric smiled. "I thought the same," he said, "until I read this verse:"

Matthew 5:44: *But I say unto you, Love your enemies, bless them that curse you, do good to them that hate you, and pray for them which despitefully use you, and persecute you;*

He pointed out that God expects practical love for our enemies so long as they remain as such. This expectation was not an unreachable goal but rather a daily reality for living. Eric's life and words so struck one boy who was struggling with resentment that years later, he returned as a missionary to the Japanese.

Eric Liddell died of a brain tumor in the camp's hospital. His last word? "Surrender."

Florence and the girls, praying for and anticipating a rapid release, knew almost nothing of Eric's circumstances. Just one week after they expected him in Canada, a letter arrived with the news of his death. Although heartbroken, Florence experienced the amazing grace of forgiveness for the

Japanese. She did not resent them, and her children observed this. One daughter testified that she was able to forgive the Japanese because of her mother's example.

Eric Liddell's family stands in stark contrast to many missionary children mentioned earlier, who reflect their parents' bitterness in their attitudes toward the churches and missionary societies they were raised in. Many parents actively sort out misunderstandings, which is fine. The problem arises when their motivation is bitterness, especially when they show this attitude in front of their kids.

POLYCARP

Polycarp (AD 80–167) is thought to be the last living man to have met and been educated by the apostles. A godly man, he believed the Bible and trusted God for the grace to obey even the most challenging verses.

Polycarp was seen as a threat by Rome, and they sent armed soldiers for him as if the old man was a thief. When they saw how old he was, they wondered why they had to make such an effort to capture him. In fact, he called for food and drink to serve them. *He had them fed!* After he was captured, the Romans told him to reject Christ. He replied, "Eighty-six years have I served Him, and He has done me no wrong. How can I blaspheme my King and my Saviour?" The Romans retaliated by burning him at the stake.[2]

Even if we have the ability to speak in tongues or the willingness to die for God, we have nothing without charity. 1 Corinthians 13:4 says, *"Charity suffereth long and is kind"*. A famous old preacher once said, "There are many people who suffer long, but very few are kind to those who made them suffer."[3]

Romans 12:17–21: *Recompense to no man evil for evil. Provide things honest in the sight of all men. If it be possible, as much as lieth in you, live peaceably with all men. Dearly beloved, avenge not yourselves, but rather give place unto wrath: for it is written, Vengeance is mine; I will repay, saith the Lord. Therefore if thine enemy hunger, feed him; if he thirst, give him drink: for in so doing thou shalt heap coals of fire on his head. Be not overcome of evil, but overcome evil with good.*

> "There are many people who suffer long, but very few are kind to those who made them suffer."

---

2 "Polycarp's Martyrdom", Christian History Institute, accessed November 21, 2015, www.christianhistoryinstitute.org/study/module/polycarp/
3 Kenneth Bedwall, *The Greatest Chapter on Love.*

LIVING LIKE JESUS

God clearly states that He will deal with the sins of man on Judgment Day. We should pray that our enemies can escape this by finding Christ. In the case of Christians who have done us wrong, we should pray they make right with God so they are not "saved as by fire." When Jesus cleansed the temple with a whip, He showed a glimpse of God's vengeance coming to the unsaved. But our job is to overcome evil with good, using love rather than vengeance to reprove and correct.

The Next Step

BIBLICAL FREEDOM FROM A BITTER HEART

As the fable goes, a miller took his son and donkey to the market. The miller started out riding the donkey and people exclaimed, "Cruel man, riding himself while his son walks." He got down and let his son ride. Then people shouted, "What a lazy son, to ride while his poor old father walks." So both father and son rode, and people then cried, "Cruelty to animals—the poor donkey!" So both got down and carried the donkey on a pole, causing everyone that passed to laugh at them. Finally, all three walked and people shook their heads; "What fools to have a donkey and not ride it."

I once arranged a group game at a family camp in South Africa that involved two teams throwing eggs at each other. People complained about it, so next time I decided to not play the game—and they still complained.

Please all, and you will please none. As Jesus said:

Luke 7:33–35: *For John the Baptist came neither eating* *bread nor drinking wine; and ye say, He hath a devil. The Son of man is come eating and drinking; and ye say, Behold a gluttonous man, and a winebibber, a friend of publicans and sinners! But wisdom is justified of all her children.*

As important as it is to obey Scripture, a Christian must also be careful not to go beyond it. Christ did not ask forgiveness of each person who disliked Him, and we need not either.

Romans 12:18: *If it be possible, as much as lieth in you, live peaceably with all men.*

Note that Paul says "if possible"—for sometimes it is impossible. Some preachers believe that you are to take the blame for every disagreement or offense someone has with you. But that would be unnecessary in the cases of the donkey, the egg game, or many other interactions with fellow men.

Throughout the Bible, most commands have to be compared to the rest of Scripture, or else they become unbalanced in the application. For instance, Jesus preached that we should pray in secret (Matthew 6), yet He prayed before a multitude during the feeding of the five thousand (John 6). God's intent was not that we should be legalistic over details, but rather that we should not pray to be seen of men. So it is with forgiveness; we mustn't run away with the concept before studying God's proper application. We must keep this especially in mind for the next steps of forgiveness: reconciliation and restitution.

When someone is bitter toward us, how should we pursue peace? If we have wronged someone, how do we make it right?

RECONCILIATION

The cross is both horizontal and vertical. Our relationship with God is important, but so are the relationships with our fellow men. In fact, our human relationships frequently reflect our relationship with God—especially in the area of forgiveness. God commands reconciliation when necessary, and we must be sure that we aren't the ones making that impossible.

Reconciliation: *The act of reconciling, or the state of being reconciled; reconcilement; restoration to harmony; renewal of friendship.*[1]

Reconciling: *Bringing into favor and friendship after variance; bringing to content or satisfaction; showing to be consistent; adjusting; making to agree.*

Of course, we are to show love to fellow men instead of nurturing bitterness. Nonetheless, there are cases where rec-

---

1 *American Dictionary of the English Language*, 1828 Ed., *s.vv.* "reconciliation, reconciling, restitution."

onciliation is not an option. No Christian had to go to Hitler and say, "Not only do I forgive you, but I would also like to start a business with you." Forgiveness is separate from reconciliation, with the second not necessarily following the first. The Bible however commands:

Matthew 5:23–26: *Therefore if thou bring thy gift to the altar, and there rememberest that thy brother hath ought against thee; Leave there thy gift before the altar, and go thy way; first be reconciled to thy brother, and then come and offer thy gift. Agree with thine adversary quickly, whiles thou art in the way with him; lest at any time the adversary deliver thee to the judge, and the judge deliver thee to the officer, and thou be cast into prison. Verily I say unto thee, Thou shalt by no means come out thence, till thou hast paid the uttermost farthing.*

This command can be misused if not obeyed in the context of the rest of Scripture. The person to reconcile must have something legitimate against you that can be made right. If a Satanist has ought against you, you don't have to apologize and join his coven. Because they preached truth, Jeremiah, Ezekiel, Paul, and Jesus had many enemies with whom they could not be reconciled while still remaining faithful. Of course we should not be personally bitter against these people, but we cannot live in peace with everyone while living and preaching truth. We can love them, but we cannot walk side by side with them and do the things they do.

The emphasis in Matthew 5:23 is on the words *brother* and *ought*. In other words, if a Christian brother actually has something legitimate against you, then you should be reconciled. However, you owe no burden of reconciliation if the issue is a false misperception or based on an illogical reason. If someone dislikes the fact you bake cookies, that is their problem. Show him love, but don't stop giving your children cookies! "Ought" does not include imaginary offenses. If I wanted a million dollars from a friend but didn't get a dime, there would be no basis for reconciliation. However, if he had stolen that million dollars from me, he would certainly have "ought" to reconcile.

Depending on the circumstances, you should not necessarily be reconciled to one person at the cost of your relationship with someone else. Reconciliation with a Satanist or worldly Christian would be at the cost of your relationship with God. You can show them love, but continue to distance yourself in practical areas.

Romans 14:21: *It is good neither to eat flesh, nor to drink wine, nor any thing whereby thy brother stumbleth, or is offended, or is made weak.*

We must use common sense with this verse. Jesus recognized that whether He came eating or fasting, someone would be offended. In this verse, Paul directs us not to do things with certain Christians that could stagger their own faith or create bitterness between us. This concept has limits in light of Scripture and practicality, since two different people can be offended by opposite things. Generally, we should not please one person by offending another.

Jude 23: *And others save with fear, pulling them out of the fire; hating even the garment spotted by the flesh.*

Reconciliation should never occur at an unbiblical cost. You should not be reconciled to your enemy at the cost of your wife or children. I know of situations where a family was hurt spiritually and emotionally because of a continued relationship with an outsider.

I remember a fellow missionary with whom I worked for a year and a half; he alienated people everywhere. My problem was that I continuously reconciled with him while he continued to offend others. Once he left, suddenly more souls were saved and God's message more easily reached others. I realized my mistake too late; I should have lovingly stopped work-

> *Reconciliation should never occur at an unbiblical cost.*

ing with him. Being selfless can in reality be quite selfish. Imagine if someone gave away all his store inventory in the name of being selfless, and then his employees lost their jobs when he went bankrupt. Love to one person can result in hate for another. If I opened my home to a rebel and he led my children astray, then my reconciliation with the rebel would be wrong.

Reconciliation with legalistic friends who adhere to extra-biblical rules can be spiritually harmful to others. Peter tried to maintain friendship with the Jewish Christians who were expecting the Gentile Christians to keep the law of feasts, Sabbaths, and circumcision. But by maintaining a relationship with them, he harmed his friendship with the Gentile Christians. The apostle Paul rebuked him:

Galatians 2:14: *But when I saw that they walked not uprightly according to the truth of the gospel, I said unto Peter before them all, If thou, being a Jew, livest after the manner of Gentiles, and not as do the Jews, why compellest thou the Gentiles to live as do the Jews?*

If any man has a legitimate grudge against us, we should be reconciled. If a relationship has been broken down through misunderstandings and false information, we should humble ourselves and pursue healing. Their response to us is between them and God; rejecting your reconciliation is their problem. Don't make the mistake of saying something like, "I am sorry for what I did, even though you were wrong because…" Your job is to be repentant, not to downplay your actions through comparison to others. However, if they are sinning or unnecessarily hurting others, we should give them the truth in love so long as our purpose is not to minimize our own sin.

RECONCILIATION WITHOUT RECIPROCATION

When someone that we have wronged is not doing their part, we should try to be reconciled, especially with family and fellow Christians. I know of a man who often became angry and even threw things around. His son told me that for years he thought this meant he did not have to make any effort to honor his father. God finally broke his heart, and he realized that if his father did not reach out to him, he should reach out to his father. After he took time to show his father love and respect, the two were able to establish a wonderful relationship.

I have another friend whose father became a drunk, left his wife, and chose a life of immorality. My friend fasted many days for his dad. One day, his father came to a Christian meeting, and my friend sat next to him. In front of all those people, he put his arm around his father's neck in love. It was as if he was saying, "Where I can, I am going to honor my dad." Sometimes, we cannot be friends in certain practical areas such as watching TV and drinking with a family member who does those things. Yet we can be reconciled when it does not clash with our relationship with God.

COMMON SENSE

The world's relationships are frequently messed up; we need much common sense when dealing with them. Reconciliation need not—or should not—happen when the other party does not want friendship or if friendship would lead us away from God. Sometimes, love and forgiveness needs to happen from a distance. We do not need to feel guilty when our friendship is not returned; simply stay free from bitterness and look elsewhere to extend love.

One boy cried as he told me how his Satanist father would beat him if he spoke against his rituals. With such a father, he honored him with forgiveness but also chose to live elsewhere, with Christians. Clearly this is a last resort; we must exercise common sense in all cases. There is no need to leave our parents because they make mistakes and occasionally get angry. Jesus said,

Matthew 10:34–36: *Think not that I am come to send*

peace on earth: I came not to send peace, but a sword. For I am come to set a man at variance against his father, and the daughter against her mother, and the daughter in law against her mother in law. And a man's foes shall be they of his own household.

Often two spouses will build a wall of grudges between each other. Both will then wait for the other to humble themselves before showing love again. God, however, expects us to humble ourselves and seek reconciliation regardless of the other's actions. I know one man who was cross because his wife did not honor him; however, he showed her no love that would call forth honor. Yet he did not see his own actions as sin, because he was comparing himself to others. He eventually broke before God, chose to ignore her faults, and in tears asked for her forgiveness. God worked in her heart as a result, and through time God gave them a very happy marriage.

Another story tells of two goats that came to the middle of a bridge from opposite sides. The only way for both to cross was if one goat humbled itself and knelt so the other goat could crawl over it. In God-ordained relationships, such as between a husband and wife or two Christian brothers, an argument needs one person who is willing to give up the last word.

RESTITUTION

Restitution: *The act of restoring anything to its rightful owner, or of making good, or of giving an equivalent for any loss, damage, or injury; indemnification.*

In certain situations where we have wronged others, God expects not only reconciliation but also restitution. If we have stolen, we should return the money or goods. If we have been involved with pornography, we should confess and seek freedom. However, we do not have to go through a Christian to reach God for forgiveness; we confess our sins to Him and He forgives. Yet we should make right with those we have directly wronged by not only seeking forgiveness, but also compensating for damage when possible. If we told a lie and many people still believe it, then we should tell the truth to the specific people involved.

> *An argument needs one person who is willing to give up the last word.*

God expects us to obey truth in the context of Scripture; Satan prefers to misuse truth. Many Christians believe that a guilty feeling must indicate sin. *Hogwash!* The New Testament describes a weak conscience, a seared conscience, and a defiled conscience. True Christians sometimes link their conscience to standards and ideas not of God; I have met some who experienced guilt over reading their Bible or a desire for marriage. God eventually set them free. Satan has convinced some Christians they can't be right with God unless they list every sin they've ever committed, or confess to man each time they experience guilt. God simply wants Christians to maintain a clear conscience. Reconciliation and restitution do not mean we need an earthly priest to be forgiven, for Jesus is the way to God. Guilt over trivial things like washing hands before prayer is unnecessary; only once we violate actual Scriptural commands should guilt have a place. Studying the Scriptures is the only way to discover right and wrong.

Acts 24:16: *And herein do I exercise myself, to have always a conscience void of offence toward God, and toward men.*

In conclusion, remember:

- Christ is our hope and our answer to every failure.
- As we have been forgiven, so also should we forgive.
- Bitterness can be corrected by humbling ourselves, seeking forgiveness, and trusting God to restore our hearts through Jesus Christ.
- Reconciliation, when possible, is the next step of forgiveness.
- Christlikeness should be the final step of forgiveness and a Christian's greatest desire, beyond any other aspiration.

One version of Christianity mimics the Pharisees and shows goodness only to the good. Another form uses a conservative lifestyle to cloak much hypocrisy. These hypocrites would probably never shoot a person with a gun, but they shoot people emotionally with their gossip, lying, and un-Christlike business dealings. On the outside, these people can dress conservatively and adhere to commendable beliefs, but inwardly they are consumed by bitterness. More people are hurt by their resentful words than are often hurt by soldiers in actual war. My father once said, "Holiness is Christ, or it is heresy." Conservative standards are good, but if they do not reflect what is on the inside, they mean nothing.

And then, there is the Christianity that seeks Christlikeness. Which do you have? Which do you want? And which are you willing to strive for?

I took private tennis lessons when I was seven years old. When the lady hit the ball over the net to me, I would send the ball flying as hard and high as possible over the tall fence behind her. I was rarely able to resist this temptation, and sent the ball into the neighbor's garden far more often than inside the court.

> *"Holiness is Christ, or it is heresy."*

God sends His word like a tennis ball across the court.

You can either keep the ball in play, or you can hit it away into the neighbor's garden and end the game. God has given you His Son and His word to obey. Will you humble yourself to forgive, reconcile, make restitution, and love as He commands?

Isaiah 66:2: *For all those things hath mine hand made, and all those things have been, saith the LORD: but to this man will I look, even to him that is poor and of a contrite spirit, and trembleth at my word.*

CONTACT THE AUTHOR

www.roydanielfamily.com

danielfamilytalk@gmail.com